MY FIRST
WORD BOOK

Venice Shone

MY FIRST
WORD BOOK

BARNES
&NOBLE
BOOKS
NEW YORK

For Rod and Annie

Illustrations copyright © Venice Shone 1993

This edition published by Barnes & Noble, Inc.,
by arrangement with Orchard Books

1999 Barnes & Noble Books

ISBN 0-7607-1228-X

Printed in China

99 00 01 02 03 MP 9 8 7 6 5 4 3 2 1

C&C

Contents

Clothes

vest

pants

dressing gown

pajamas

hanger

slippers

shoes

socks

tights

t-shirt

dungarees

sweater

pinafore

skirt

jacket

belt

tie

sandals

trousers

cardigan

dress

tracksuit

shorts

shirt

shoes

hat

cap

gym shoes

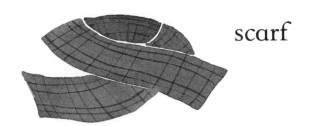
scarf

hair ribbon

coat

party dress

rain hat

anorak

rubber boots

mittens

raincoat

Toys

teaset

picture books

teddy bear

plane

doll

doll's carriage

doll's clothes

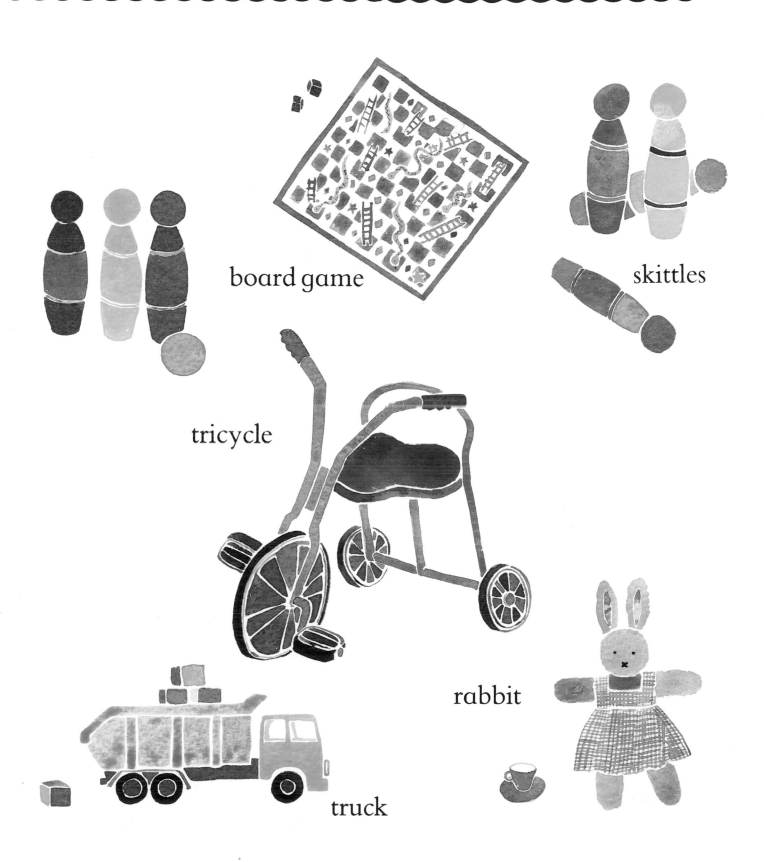

board game

skittles

tricycle

rabbit

truck

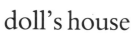

doll's house

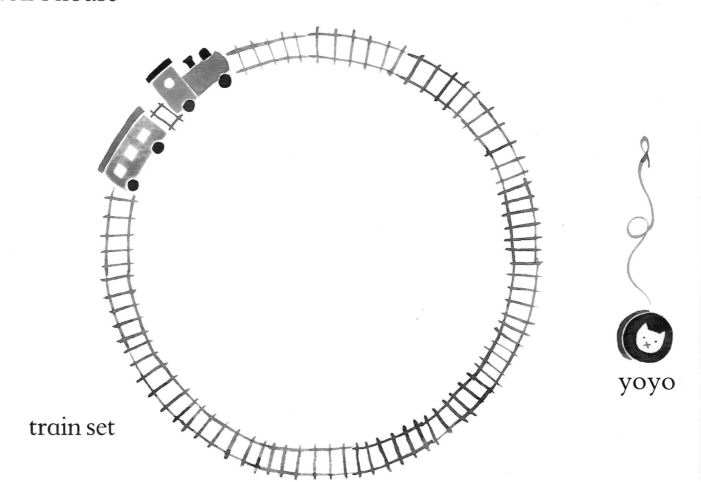

train set

yoyo

toy fort

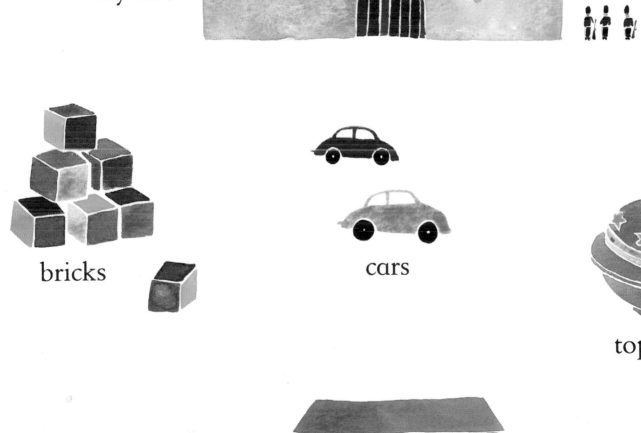

bricks

cars

top

toy animals

Noah's ark

13

Mealtimes

spoon

egg cup

mug

pie

teapot

glass

napkin

fork

plate

sugar

salt

pepper

bread

milk jug

cup and saucer

butter

coffee pot

jam

knife

In the Kitchen

oven glove

jug

kettle

ladle

spatula

frying pan

saucepan

rolling pin

mixing bowl

wooden spoon

colander

recipe book

whisk

can opener

pastry cutters

cheese grater

lemon squeezer

Cleaning Things

rubber gloves

washing-up liquid

shoe polish

shoe cleaning brush

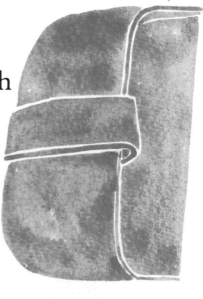

dustpan

brush

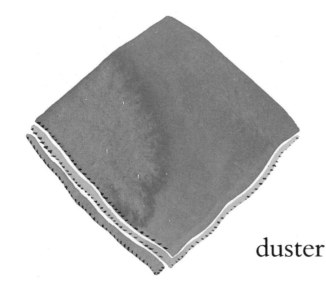

duster

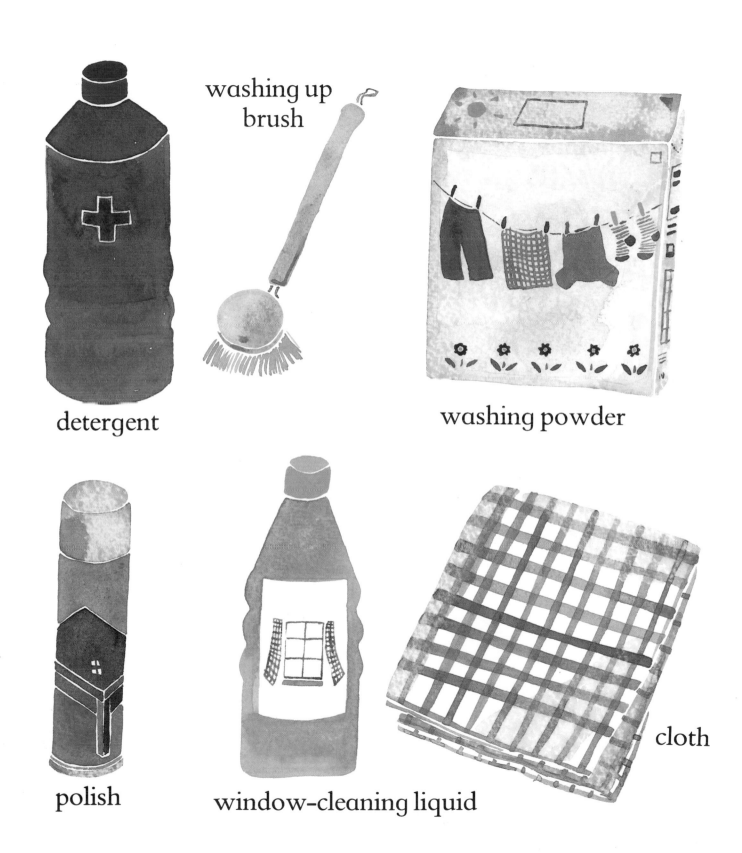

detergent

washing up brush

washing powder

polish

window-cleaning liquid

cloth

In the House

telephone

television

hairdryer

iron

ironing board

alarm clock

radio

laundry basket

washing machine

stove

fridge

cushion

sofa

carpet

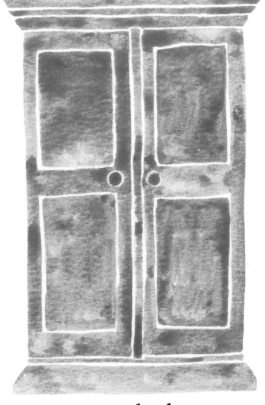

picture

lamp

wardrobe

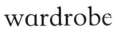

chest of drawers

bed

chair

vase

table

bath

sink

toilet

23

In the Bathroom

duck

bath brush

toothpaste

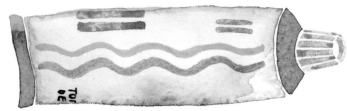

bath bag

toothbrush

perfume

bubble bath

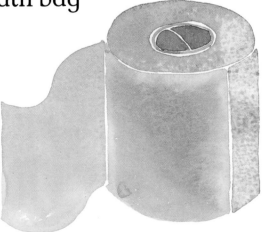
toilet roll

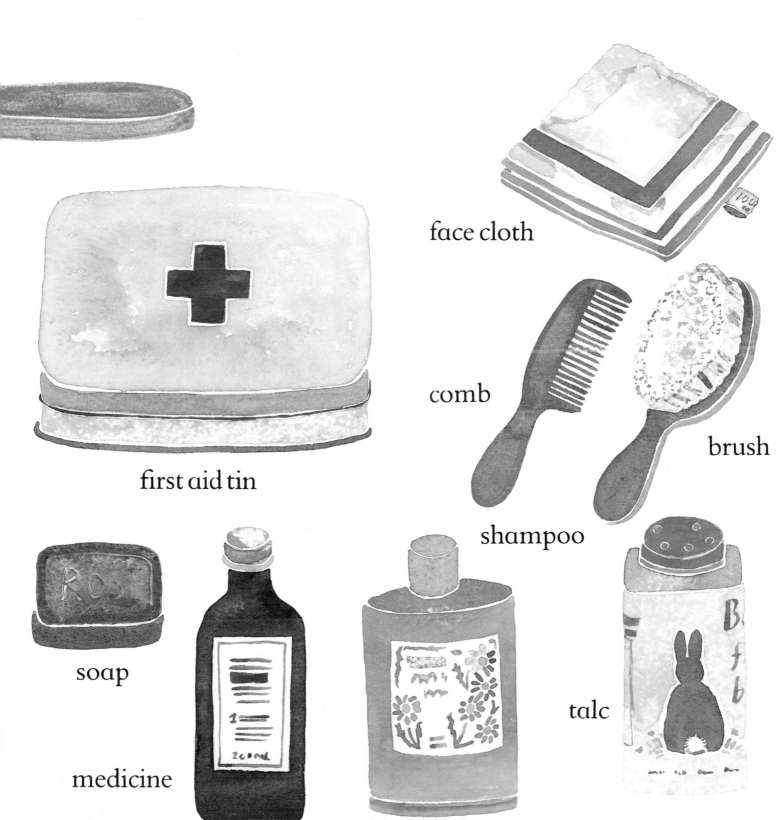

face cloth

first aid tin

comb

brush

shampoo

soap

medicine

talc

Little Things

handkerchief

button

keys

penknife

dice

matches

needle

pin

ring

thread

candy

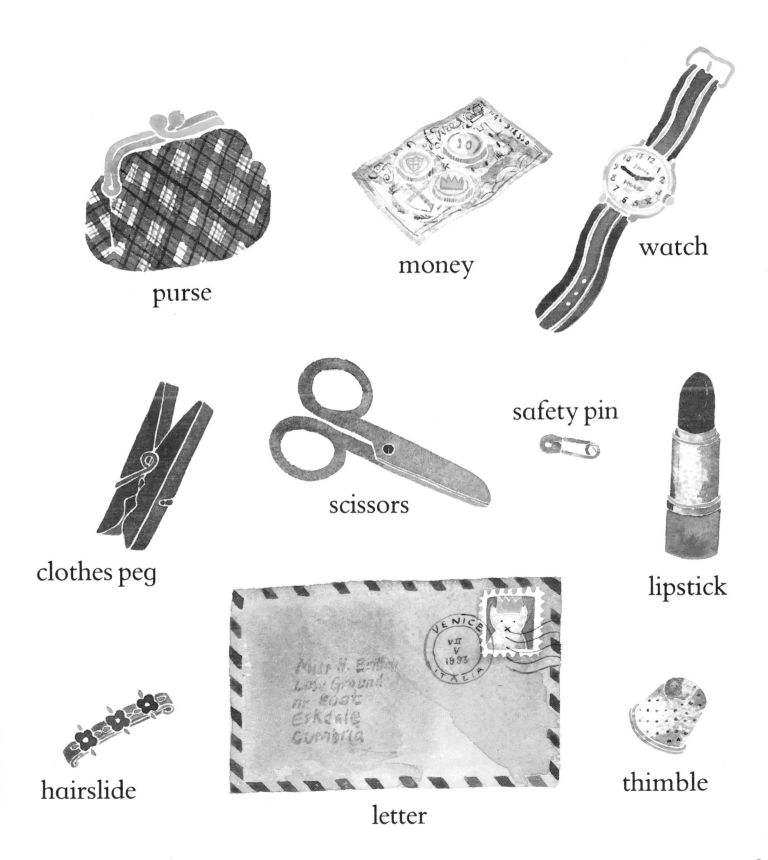

purse

money

watch

clothes peg

scissors

safety pin

lipstick

hairslide

letter

thimble

Tools

bucket

paint

paintbrush

scrubbing brush

painting tray

white spirit

stepladder

roller

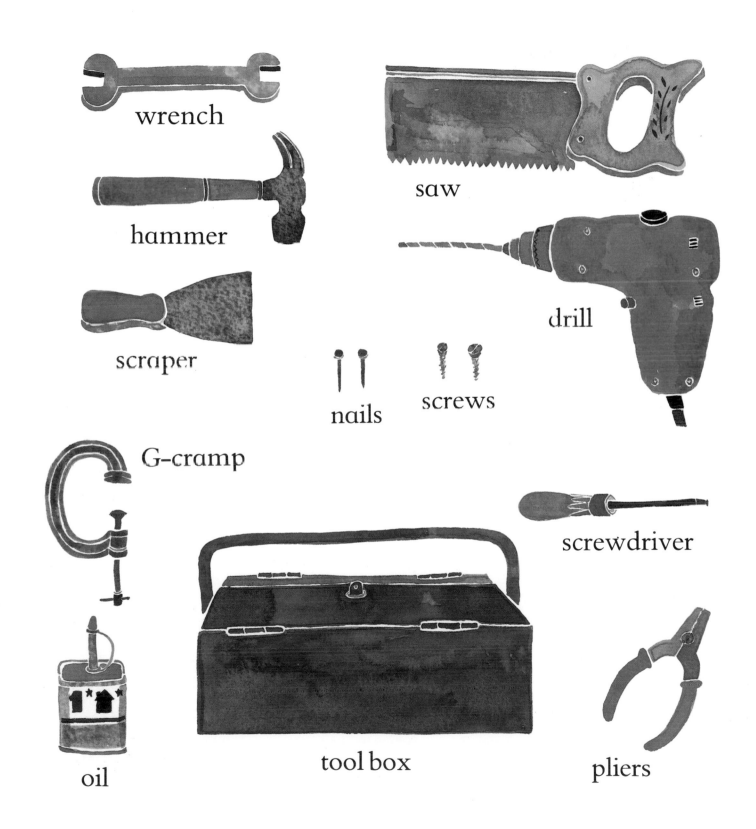

wrench

hammer

scraper

saw

drill

nails

screws

G-cramp

screwdriver

oil

tool box

pliers

In the Garden

sieve

fork

trowel

big fork

rake

spade

hose

flowerpot

plant

flowers

snail

twine

ladybug

bec

seeds

watering can

butterfly

secateurs

Animals

dog

cat

rabbit

mouse

goldfish

bird

duck

hen

cow

sheep

horse

goat

pig

elephant

camel

tiger

giraffe

lion

kangaroo

bear

monkey

parrot

snake

crocodile

penguin

whale

Buildings

apartment building

windmill

tent

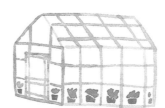

igloo

cottage

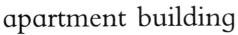

greenhouse

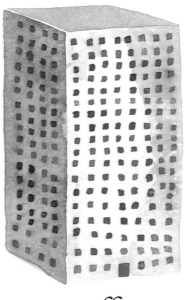

office

barn

factory

church

kennel

house

garden shed

lighthouse

castle

Transport

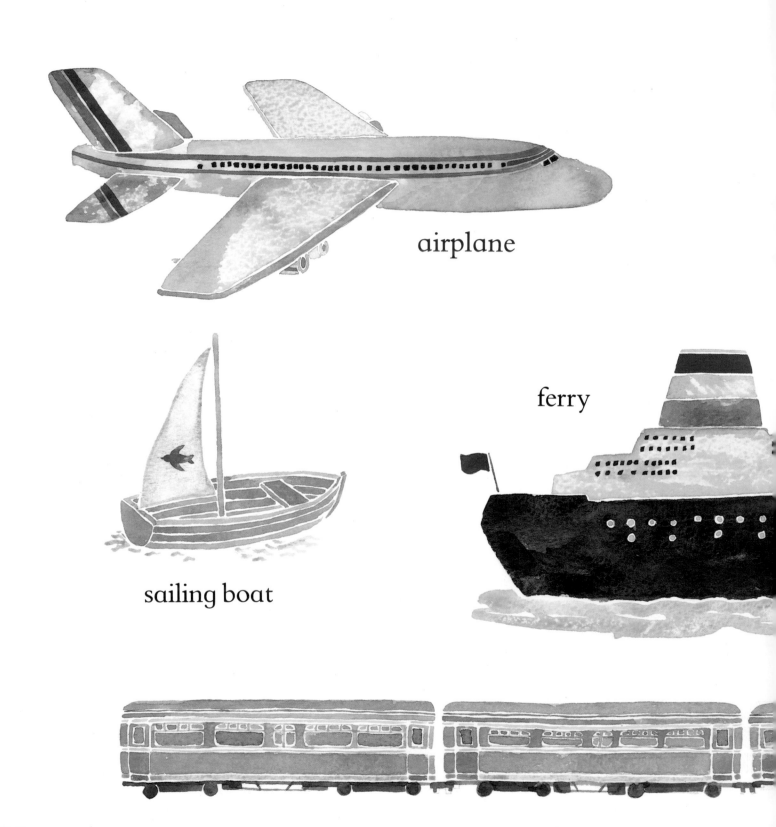

airplane

ferry

sailing boat

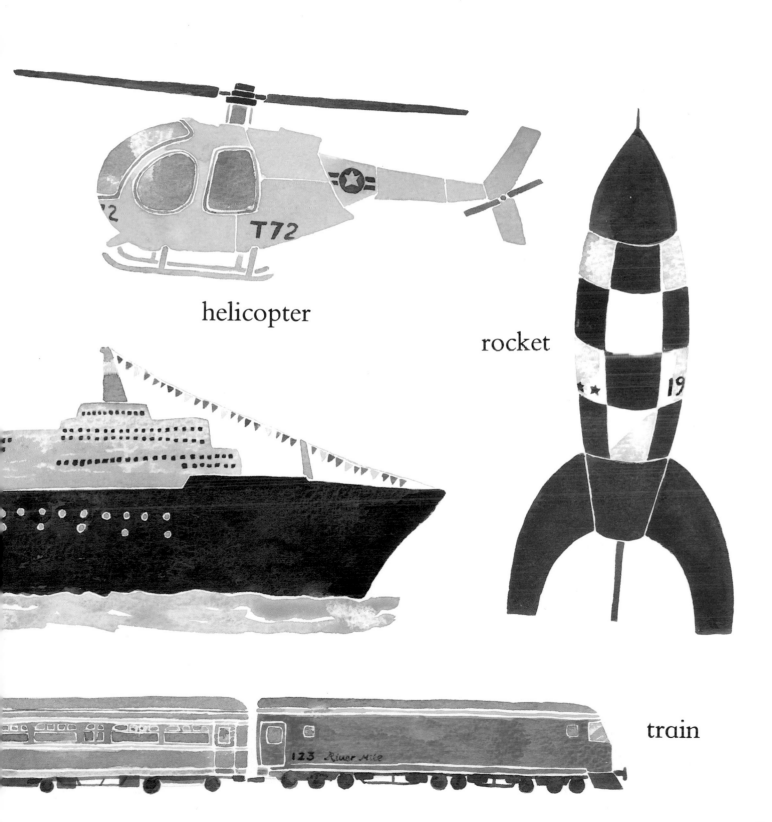

helicopter

rocket

train

coach

truck

racing car

tractor

taxi

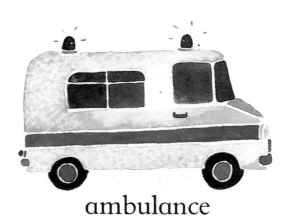

ambulance

motorcycle

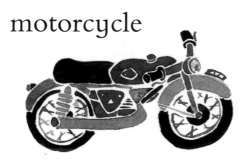

motorbike

trailer

fire engine

police car

break-down truck

car

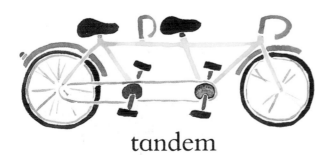

tandem

bicycle

Shopping

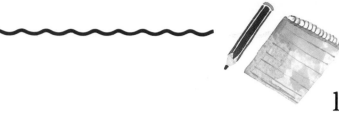

basket

bread

rolls

list

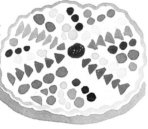

paper bag

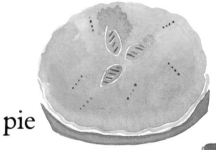

pie

cakes

fruit tart

cereal

milk

butter

tea

coffee

eggs

yogurt

tin

pasta

flour

sugar

oil

honey

jam

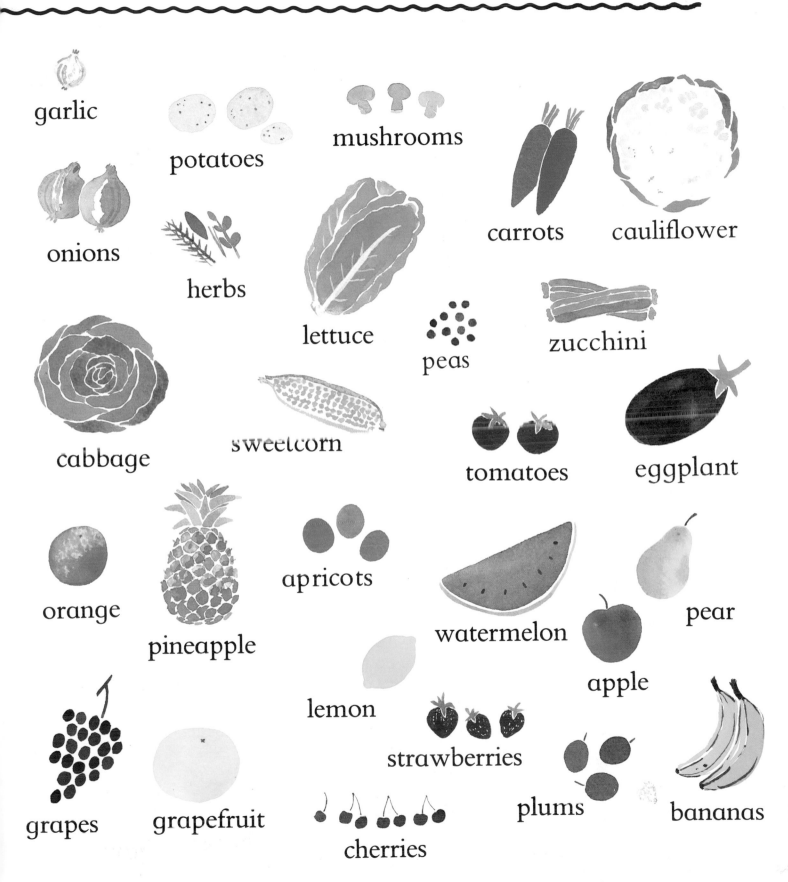

garlic

potatoes

mushrooms

carrots

cauliflower

onions

herbs

lettuce

peas

zucchini

cabbage

sweetcorn

tomatoes

eggplant

orange

pineapple

apricots

watermelon

pear

apple

lemon

strawberries

grapes

grapefruit

cherries

plums

bananas

43

In the Street

butcher

fresh fish

vegetable stall

ice cream stall

bakery

café

flower stall

news-stand

In the Park

roller skates

tennis ball

tennis racket

boat

carriage

pigeon

football

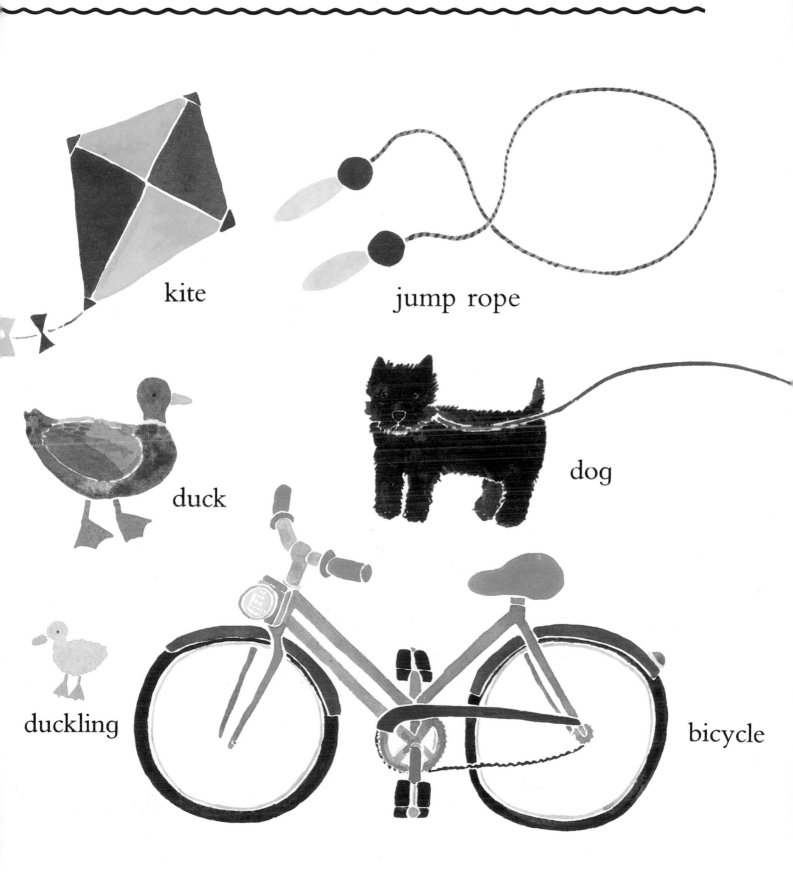

kite

jump rope

duck

dog

duckling

bicycle

At the Seaside

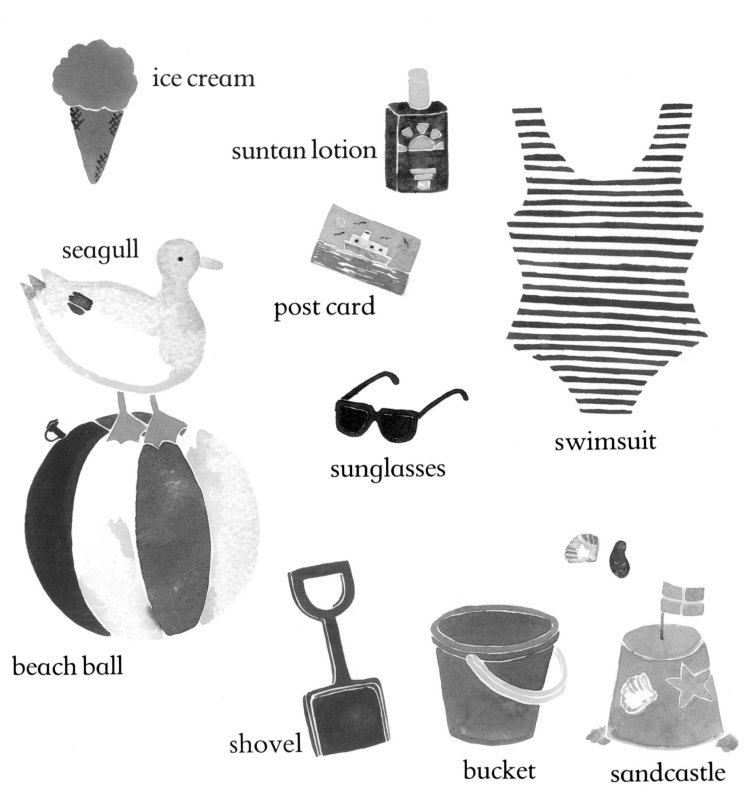

ice cream

suntan lotion

post card

swimsuit

seagull

sunglasses

beach ball

shovel

bucket

sandcastle

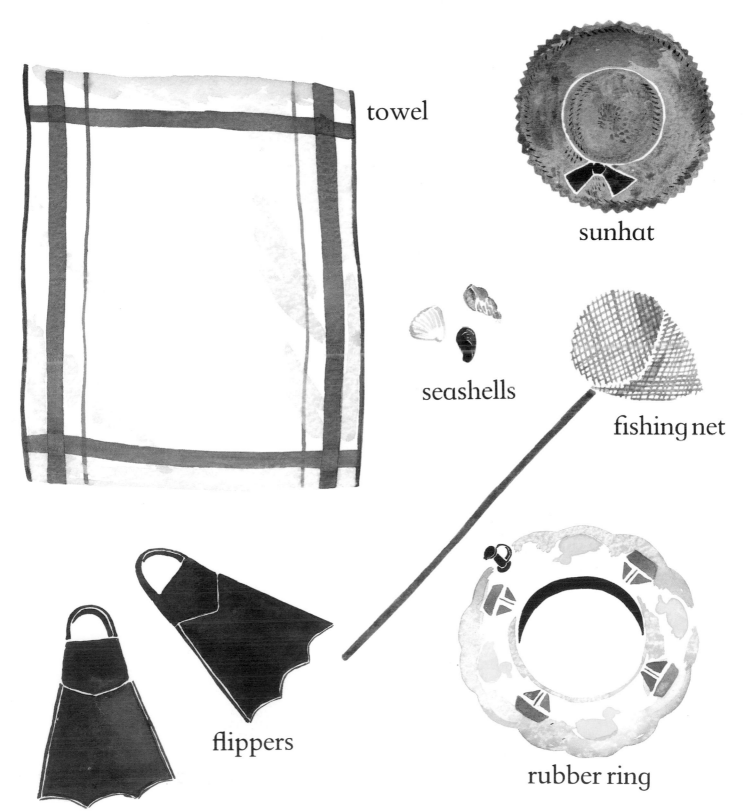

towel

sunhat

seashells

fishing net

flippers

rubber ring

49

Party Time ~~~~~~~~

balloon

paper hat

box of chocolates

fruit juice

cake

straw

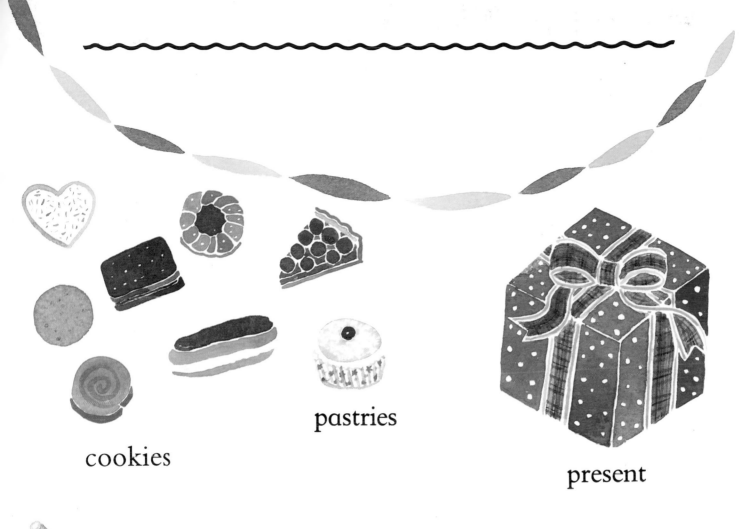

cookies

pastries

present

whistle

champagne

bouquet

Musical Instruments

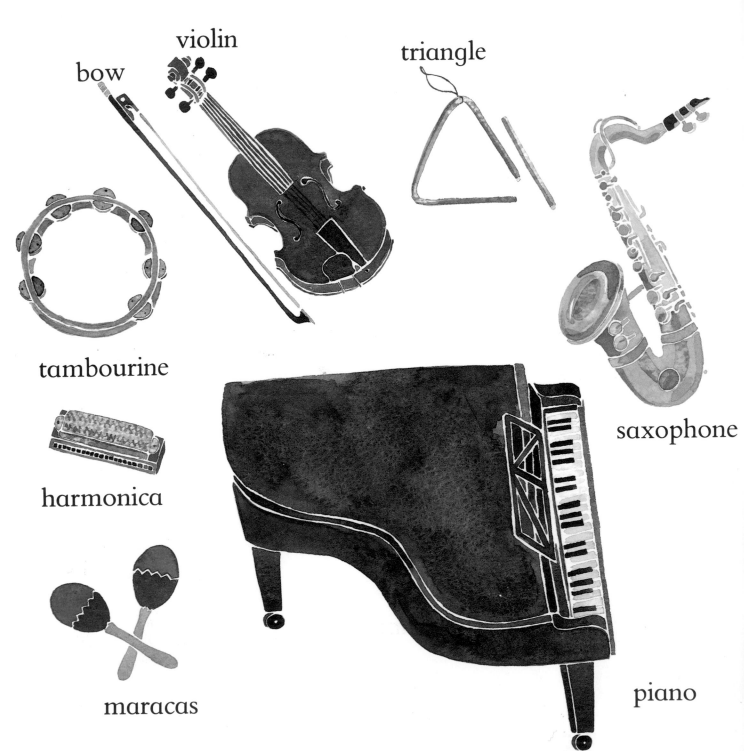

bow

violin

triangle

saxophone

tambourine

harmonica

maracas

piano

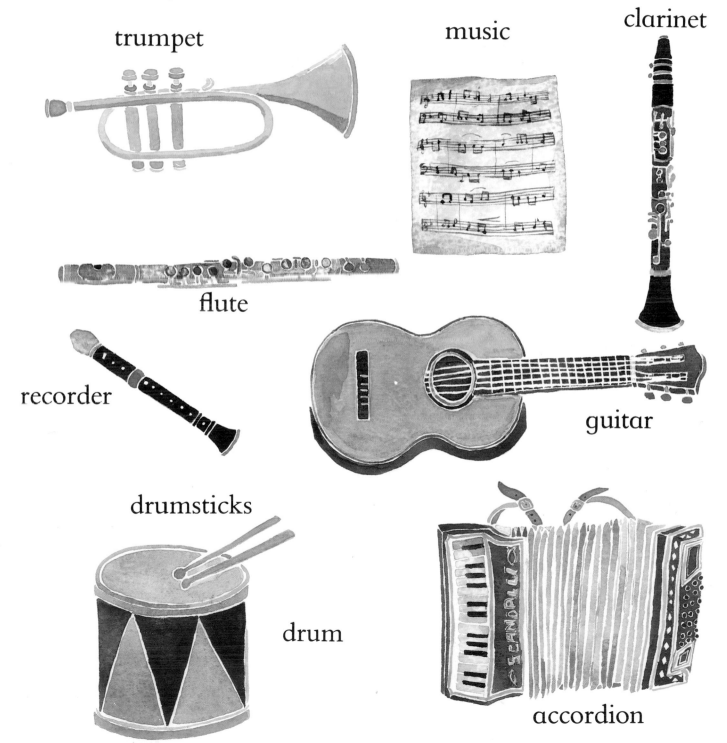

trumpet

music

clarinet

flute

recorder

guitar

drumsticks

drum

accordion

At School

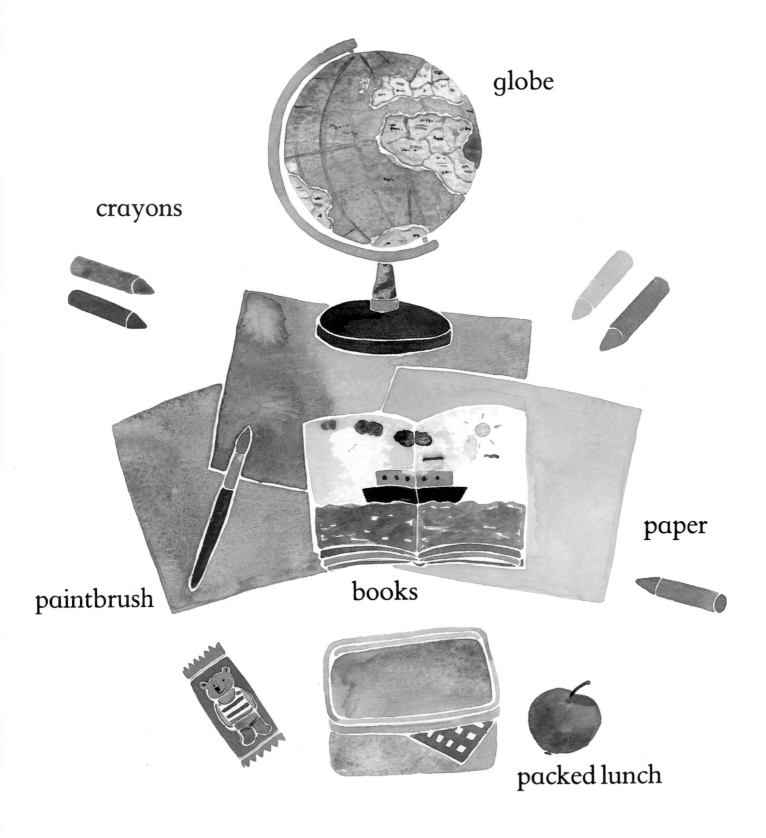

globe

crayons

paintbrush

books

paper

packed lunch

school bag

glue

exercise book

$2 + 8 =$
$5 + 7 =$
$10 + 6 =$
$11 + 4 =$

pencil sharpener

ink

eraser

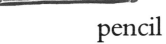

pencil

pen

ruler

Colours

orange

red

blue

yellow

white

black

silver

gold

grey

green

purple

pink

brown

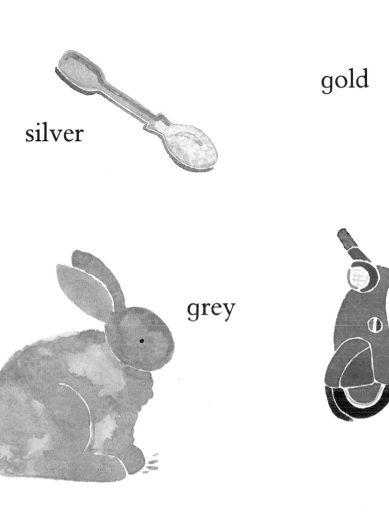

Seasons

spring

summer

sun

rainbow

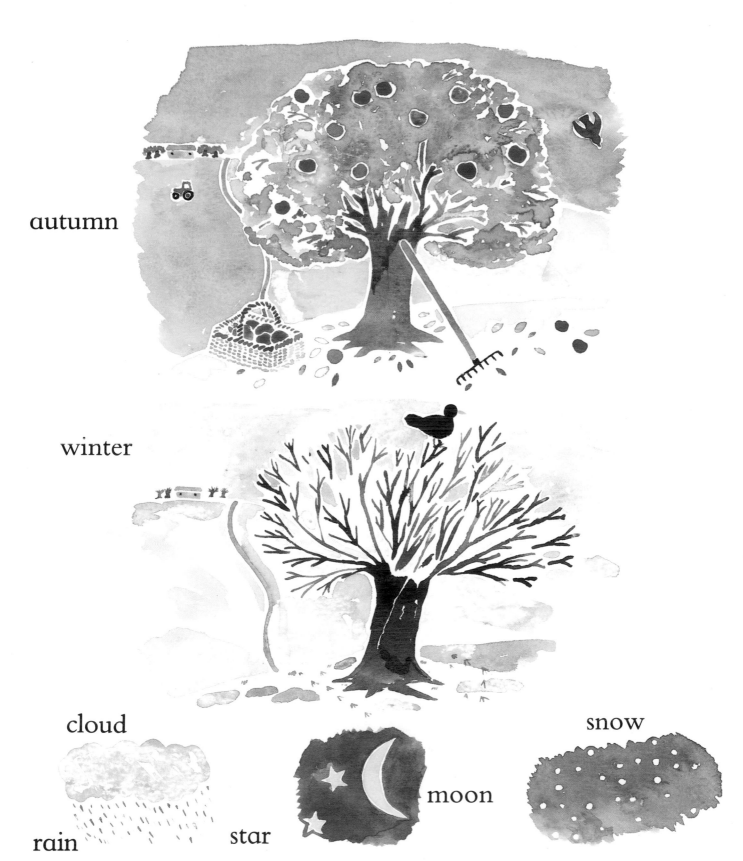

autumn

winter

cloud

rain

star

moon

snow

Numbers

1 one

2 two

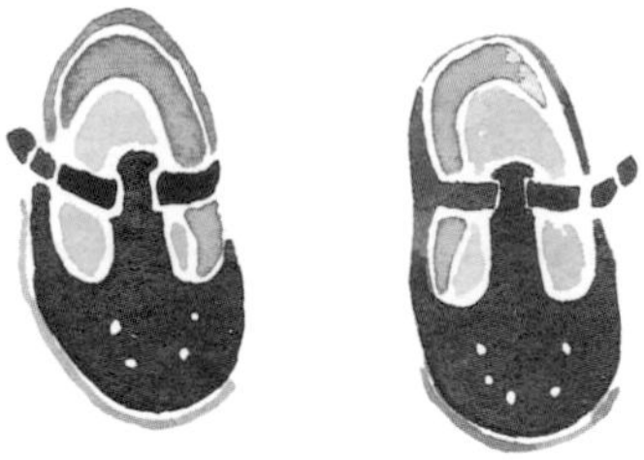

3 three

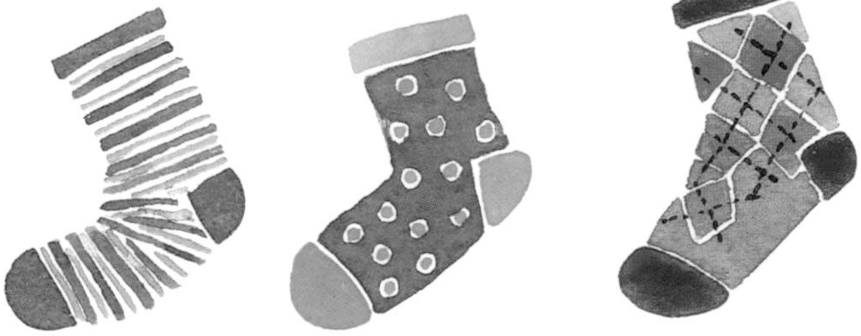

4 four

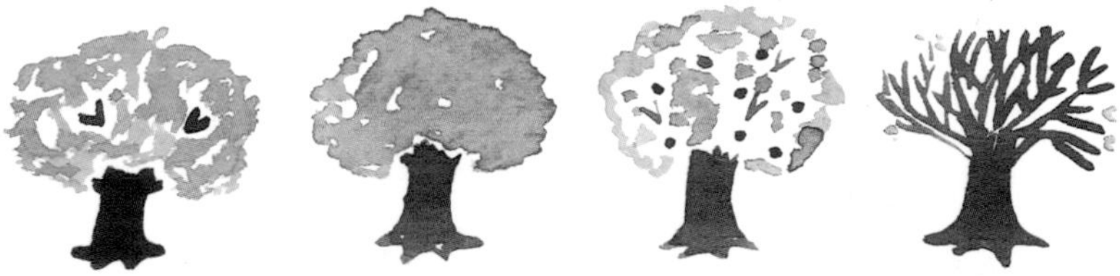

5 five

6 six

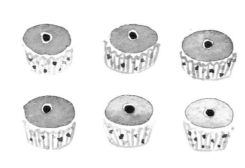

7 seven

8 eight

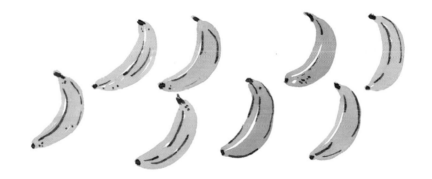

9 nine

10 ten

20 twenty

30 thirty

40 forty

50 fifty

60 sixty

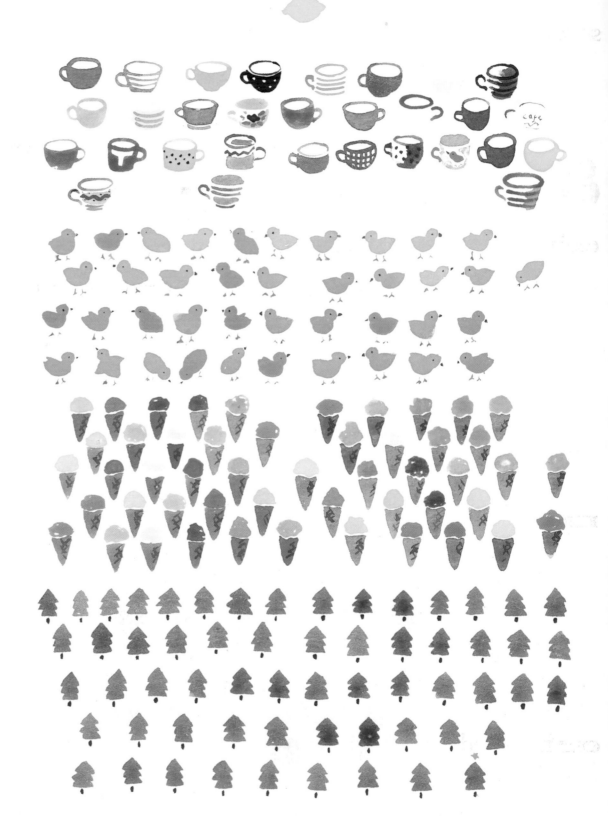

70

seventy

80

eighty

90

ninety

100

one hundred

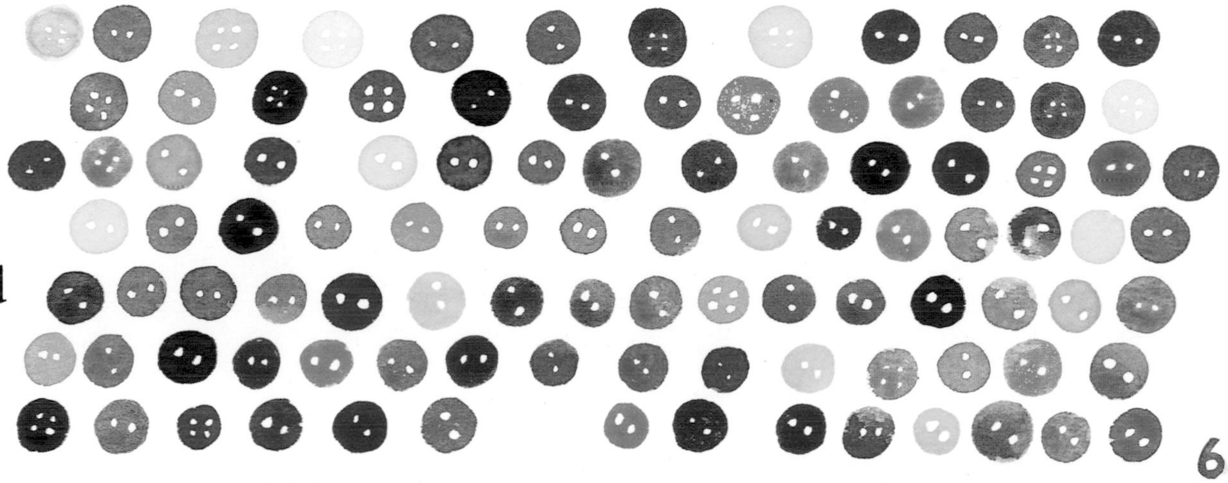

Months

January

 February

 March

 April

 May

June

 July

 August

 September

 October

 November

 October

December

Days

 Monday

Tuesday  Wednesday

Thursday

 Friday

 Saturday

Sunday